Recreation Ground

Tom Phillips was born in Buckinghamshire in 1964 but has spent most of his adult life in Bristol where he lives with his wife and two children. A freelance journalist and writer, he has worked as a producer in local radio, edited *Venue* magazine and contributed to a variety of other publications, including *The Guardian*, *Contemporary Review*, *Tribune*, *Plays International* and *Exeunt*. His plays have been produced in Bristol and Bath, and range from community musical *Concorde Stories* for BBC Radio Bristol to one-man show *I Went To Albania* at Bristol Old Vic.

Two Rivers Press First Collection Series
Kate Behrens, *The Beholder* (2012)
Tom Phillips, *Recreation Ground* (2012)

The First Collection Series was launched in 2012 to provide an opportunity for emerging poets, already visible on the reading circuit or in pamphlet form, to have a debut, self-contained statement collaboratively shaped, edited, designed and published.

Also by Two Rivers Poets:
Paul Bavister, *Miletree* (1996)
Paul Bavister, *Glass* (1998)
Paul Bavister, *The Prawn Season* (2002)
Kate Behrens, *The Beholder* (2012)
Adrian Blamires, *The Effect of Coastal Processes* (2005)
Adrian Blamires, *The Pang Valley* (2010)
Joseph Butler, *Hearthstone* (2006)
Jane Draycott and Lesley Saunders, *Christina the Astonishing* (1998)
Jane Draycott, *Tideway* (2002)
John Froy, *Eggshell: A Decorator's Notes* (2007)
David Greenslade, *Zeus Amoeba* (2009)
A. F. Harrold, *Logic and the Heart* (2004)
A. F. Harrold, *Postcards from the Hedgehog* (2007)
A. F. Harrold, *Flood* (2009)
Ian House, *Cutting the Quick* (2005)
Gill Learner, *The Agister's Experiment* (2011)
Kate Noakes, *The Wall Menders* (2009)
Victoria Pugh, *Mrs Marvellous* (2008)
Peter Robinson, *English Nettles and Other Poems* (2010)
Peter Robinson (ed.), *Reading Poetry: An Anthology* (2011)
Peter Robinson (ed.), *A Mutual Friend: Poems for Charles Dickens* (2012)
Lesley Saunders, *Her Leafy Eye* (2009)
Lesley Saunders, *Cloud Camera* (2012)
Susan Utting, *Houses Without Walls* (2006)
Susan Utting, *Fair's Fair* (2012)

Recreation Ground
Tom Phillips

TWO RIVERS PRESS

First published in the UK in 2012 by Two Rivers Press
7 Denmark Road, Reading RG1 5PA.
www.tworiverspress.com

© Tom Phillips 2012

The right of the poet to be identified as the author of the work
has been asserted by him in accordance with the Copyright,
Designs and Patents Act of 1988.

All rights reserved. No part of this publication may be reproduced,
stored in or introduced into a retrieval system, or transmitted,
in any form, or by any means (electronic, mechanical, photocopying,
recording or otherwise) without the prior written permission of
the publisher.

ISBN 978-1-901677-85-0

1 2 3 4 5 6 7 8 9

Two Rivers Press is represented in the UK by Inpress Ltd and
distributed by Central Books.

Cover design by Nadja Guggi using Pete Hay's illustrations.
Text design by Nadja Guggi and typeset in Janson and Parisine.

Printed and bound in Great Britain by Imprint Digital, Exeter.

For Sarra, Lydia and Samuel

By the same author:

Poetry
Burning Omaha, Firewater Press (2003)
Reversing into the Cold War, Firewater Press/Poetry Monthly (2007)

Plays
Concorde Stories (2003)
Hotel Illyria (2008)
Rose's Last Laugh (2009)
Arbeit Macht Frei (2009)
Beware of the Flowers (2010)
The Few (2010)
Man Diving (2011)
I Went To Albania (2012)

Acknowledgements
Some of the poems in *Recreation Ground* have previously appeared in *Various Artists*, *Eyewear*, *nthposition*, *Poetry Scotland*, *Poetry Monthly International* and *Nagy Vilag*. 'Life After Wartime' was published in *100 Poets Against The War* (Salt, 2003), 'Burning Omaha' in *In The Criminal's Cabinet* (nthposition, 2004), 'Fear of Flying' in *Babylon Burning* (nthposition, 2006), 'Ornithology in the Balkans' and 'The Centre, Friday' in *nothing like concrete* (University of Reading, 2011), and 'Found in the River' in *A Mutual Friend* (Two Rivers Press, 2012). 'Life After Wartime', 'Burning Omaha' and 'Portishead' also appeared in *Burning Omaha* (Firewater Press, 2003). As well as expressing gratitude to the editors of all these publications, I would particularly like to thank Peter Robinson, Tony Lewis Jones, Todd Swift, Rosemary Dun and Adrian Blamires for ongoing encouragement and help beyond the call of duty.

Contents

Life After Wartime | 1
Burning Omaha | 2
Fear of Flying | 3
Recreation Ground | 4
Not Really Climbing the Malvern Hills | 5
Just Before the Boat | 7
Dubliners on the Adriatic | 8
In the Small Museum | 10
Moving East | 11
A Trophy | 12
A Curious Friendship | 13
Ornithology in the Balkans | 14
Here After All | 15
European Union | 16
View Becoming a Poem | 17
Miles Away | 18
Changing the Geography | 20
Performance Art in Private Gardens | 21
The Chopin Question | 22
Egdon Road | 23
The Three-Day Melt | 24
So Close | 25
Found in the River | 26
The Breakage Suite | 28
Fenlanders | 30
Ellerker Gardens | 32
The Stone Platoon | 33
The Air Display | 34
Wearing Thin | 35
Disrupted Sleep | 36
Back on the Shelf | 37
Observation Carriage | 38
Playing Piano for the Folks | 39
Catching the Drift | 40

Almost There | 41
Allotment Poem | 42
Long-term Forecast | 43
The Centre, Friday | 45
Portishead | 46

Life After Wartime

Some things never change.
The garden bushes wag their beards
like arguing theologians while the orange fists
of passion fruit take cover in the leaves.
The sky aches with unmapped distances
and the sun hides nothing.
At dusk, it surrenders to the moon.

When there's small-hours muttering in the street
remember it's only someone deciding to go home or go on,
pushing the night for the last of the great good times
and into a shell-shocked morning after.

At least there's coffee again.
It takes our minds off the radio,
the smooth-voiced reassurances,
the metaphors encrusted like barnacles
on every announcement, your almost
imperceptible jump at the sound
of a pamphlet shoved through the door.

Things never change.
People wear their silence like a caul.
To bring them luck against drowning.
They were parents. Or siblings. Or both.
They are the ones that nothing surprises,
the ones who no longer look up
when a jet comes roaring in above the city,
framed against the orange sky,
picking its way among the towers.

Burning Omaha

All summer it was like a miracle,
the dust coating cars and running
your finger through sand they said
had blown in from the Sahara.
Drivers cursed. It was a summer
of talk. Of incidents, evacuations,
populations gridlocking ring roads,
four-minute warnings, the hottest season
of their Cold War. We didn't care.
We were racing through the woods
while parents stocked up on tins
and candles and stared at the radio
with palms against their throats
as if by suddenly tightening their grip
they could hold their little faith in.
There was no rain, only sand,
only sand coming down like scurf,
like unexpected snow from Archangel,
like the ashes from Omaha burning.

Fear of Flying

Every night these small-hours panics,
airliners knife into the sea,
her whispered reassurances:
Sleep, my love, it's only dreams –
until fear is strafing the ceiling
like searchlights, like a convoy
of hooded trucks out east.

Are we at war again? The papers
say nothing. Our rooms are filled
with shopping bags, unpaid bills,
traps for insomniacs, clutter.
Not one of us has any clue.
The dawn which haunts the window
is merely a trick of the light.
The man in the doorway, smoking,
checks his field of fire.

Recreation Ground

So much for making it,
cutting up the escarpment
to reach the shallow chalk crater
where, finally, the tennis courts
were out of sight and all
we had to watch were the clouds
that shaped themselves and rolled away.

We were still among the scrub
and the sheep-tracks, my first love,
when you turned an ankle
and, leaning against the slope,
looked back to where our parents
were making ready to play.

Not Really Climbing the Malvern Hills

Aiming to get away early,
not from everything exactly,
but roadworks, torn-up roundabouts,
the insistence on improvement
in continual redevelopment,
we made the first train out of Temple Meads,
barely noticing where it would take us:
the slow, stopping service to Malvern.

Twenty years since I walked this ridge
buckling out of Worcestershire,
the abrupt scarp surprised us.
Disappointment in the weather
might well have turned us home
from where fleshy rhododendra
suggested provincial Victoriana
and a tea-room waiter's sniffy air
suggested not much at all.
A whole town tilted on a slope
whose fortunes remain,
whoever's in the government:
the stiff church headstones
of those who believed
they'd paid their dues
for what they had received,
small sacrifices earning just rewards.

Only, climbing granite steps
through log-fire smoke,
we spied an unexpected geography:
stockaded new towns, arterial roads
like a railway modeller's indulgent scheme
for tunnels and impossible curves.

Chestnuts dripped rain onto gardens,
secretive addresses a long way down,
and gated gravel driveways carved up
middle England. High above them,
we watched more clouds come in
over Birmingham, then Worcester.

Each new burst swept crumpled fields,
caught us not entirely unawares
as we raced to a mossy clump of rock,
the furthest along these hills we'd reach,
mist rising behind us on untroubled streets
where nothing will change no matter what.

Just Before the Boat

At the frontier, waters glazed.
Baggage rose on the harbourside.
Old gods threatened to stand their ground.
We checked tickets, passports, nationalities.

As the roll-on-roll-off ramp came down,
chains struck thick clanking notes
and, beyond the emptying docks,
a poem, or one remembered, took their place.

Coffee and raki slipped over the bar.
We were half-frazzled by sunshine,
just so many people awaiting a boat
amongst landmark ramparts, a lighthouse.

Fifty yards down the quay,
a floating skyscraper: wall
of portholes where temporary friends
leant out, assumed their watch,
and shouted suggestions like goodbyes.

Dubliners on the Adriatic

La mia anima è a Trieste ...

I
Trieste. Trst. Tristesse.
Rustle of sea birds rising
from this doubling bay,
suggestive echoes along the Canal Grande:
here, of all places, to stumble on
Joyce among the Hapsburgs,
blind bronze staggered mid-stride.

Unhinged from its hinterland,
this polyglot port's piazza's fading
hulks outline a century's diminishment:
'the last foothold before...' etc., etc.,
(barbarism, in short),
Austria-Hungary's gravestone wedged
in the crotch of the Adriatic.

Distant Istria fumes blue in the heat.
White Miramar – from where
reluctant Maximilian despatched
for Mexico (and Manet) – plunges
foolishly above the sea,
imperial mockery mocked,
the silver, unmoving sea.

2
City of sighs,
where the wise
keep their eyes on
the empty horizon,
though no ships come
and the quays are dumb
as Franz Ferdinand
lumping up the Corso,
dead. Or the Risiera
where the Jews were killed.

3
But staggering mostly, by ill-repute,
he was, from quay to quay,
until Consul's counsel held sway,
and he teetered off to the *bahnhof*.

Under palms, under plane trees,
Joyce whistled off-key by the Chiave D'Oro,
(girls there knowing him, by ill-repute),
for his Triestine tryst with Nora.

With other tongues loose in his mouth –
Honest, Jim, she'll smell them on your breath! –
and her fresh-flustered from the Zurich train,
he fanfared her exile into his free world,
waltzed her through statued gardens,
his animated, Babelous greeting:
'Per donna, jam hors de clay.'

In the Small Museum

It can't be uncommon in this room
to imagine yourself by the desk,
by the window, seeing the street
for the first time impossibly distant.

There are five or six of us now
beneath the leader's touched-up portrait,
running over what we meant to say,
our most thorough confessions.

It's easy to do. It's all on file:
exactly who betrayed and how;
anything might fit the picture,
whatever you choose to add.

Only turn the tables and it's you
who's looking at a bruised, exhausted face.
It refuses to answer but still you ask:
'What right have you to accuse yourself?'

Moving East

Overweight terrapins
loom in silted water
on the station café windowsill
as tannoy announcements
deferring a cross-country train
defeat our phrasebook Slovak.

No doubt, when passing through,
some scion of the Hapsburgs
or Party official affected
the same amphibious boredom,
declaring, when forced,
the town to be utterly charming.

You could say that.
Below what remains of a forest
scored with out-of-season pistes,
colonnades shadow tilted streets
and greenery fringes marshal
the bounds of a modest piazza.

Or you could dissect elements
of central European picturesque.
Only now, among shrugging commuters,
you're looking back, overseen by the church,
on a branch of Tesco and, last night,
pints of Guinness in a Mexican bar.
Whatever you hoped to find,
you're not the first to get here.

A Trophy

Somewhere, a small boy's hat beneath a sofa.
Victory over all-comers marches on
the socialist-realist mosaic
of the National Historical Museum.
The traffic's rout snarls into gridlock.
A gardener upends weeds around
the tread of a captured tank.

He lost it – he can't be sure –
in the Bourgeois Deviationist Era
(unrevised captions finding
reactionary intent in spectacled faces)
or after Ottoman Feudal Resistance
and before the People's Heroic Struggle
Against Fascist Aggression.

Curators drawing on cigarettes
beneath fissured icons
rummage between exhibits
for a blue Italia football cap.
A small boy races, bare-headed,
through galleries left untended.
Like a line of beaters, we advance.

Mannequins sporting mountain dress,
Roman mosaics and torsos,
a partisan's bullet-holed jacket ...
Elsewhere, a small boy's hat's been found.
From the walls of names and headshots,
the documented dead look down.

A Curious Friendship

For Ilya

It was what? A lack of baldness
or my lavender shirt
that kept you guessing?
On the citadel's ruinous heights,
I couldn't let things be.

Who was this, asking you
to name the birds making *m*s
against the sky? Or to do
the impossible and say
who laid those flowers
for *the unknown*?

Satellite photos trace the road
through vast grey shoals
of alluvial deposits,
or there's the lahuta's strain
on recordings from the stage
that rusted behind us.

Two years, she said, the other day,
and still I can't reach back
to where you held my son
at an Ottoman gun-slit,
our cigarettes stubbed on the wall.

Ornithology in the Balkans

It wasn't the Muslim weddings that took your eye
on that alluvial floodplain so much
as bent-wire cages under every tree,
goldfinches' less than common soliciting
beside trapped black squirrels and a dove.
At *xhiro* hour, along streets of dark stairwells,
the hawkers were out, their not-so-fair trade
luring buyers who swooped on bargains,
took promises of health and long life
as more than hot air. On the fly,
you might have been taken in
by flashes of iridescence or plain song.
In the mountains of another country,
the rumoured eagles were predominantly crows.

But here, above the disputed town,
its castle flaunts a history of sieges
in so many collapsing terraces.
The milk-white dribble between stones,
they say, seeps from the breasts
of a wife immured to satisfy gods.

Across the promontory's ruined terrain,
we were trying to work out which wall
had belonged to which religion
when, against the faithless sky,
a squadron flew in: dandy pigeons
stumbling around, wild birds
hunting for a roost in feathery galoshes.

Here After All

For Peter Robinson

Beneath pink stucco facades,
slung hocks of purple ham,
we milled on the threshold
of another couple's wedding day
among guests who themselves
arrived too early or late.

After three weeks brought us as close
as failed calls' repetitive pips last night,
there it was, as far as we'd get,
a perfect lack of coincidence.
A distracted passer-by let on
he wasn't sure if he'd seen you in days.

Was it time to turn for home?
Tram cables, dusty sunlight,
names I almost recognised
(except we'd never been this way before)
were threatening to become
occasions to be spoken of
at a later date.

Tourists twice over on borrowed ground
and short of a guide-book suggestion,
we might just have left
on a convenient afternoon train.
I was trying the family's patience
until – as if by chance –
gravel paths through the Parco Ducale
brought us out of shade,
to the lip of a fountain cistern
as dark carp rose where you said they'd be,
nosing the surface, here for all to see.

European Union

At first it might have been coincidence
that we heard so many car horns
shifting through the Doppler effect,
or checked in at hotels where girls
in Sunday best held hands and sang
interminable folk tunes.

Only, the following day, new couples
emerged from a scaffolded church
with candles lit, and family groups
assembled in a park for photographs
where filigree blossom coincidentally
obscured the Stalinist backdrop.

Thirty, forty weddings eased
from municipal ceremonies to pose
beneath late-flowering cherry trees,
anticipated pleasures, and advice
they'd hardly need, being of an age
when all has seemed so changed.

Such innocence again around the square,
these brand new starts, this expectation,
Romanian sunlight on dove-grey dresses.

View Becoming a Poem

A great thing it might be,
although for the moment
I'm no longer convinced
amongst beer cans, ash-flecks,
potholes of yawning vowels.

Then again, set a few careful words
against this photocopied leaflet
from Tourist Information,
picked up, glanced at, left.

Rashers of bacon in a floury bap
extend towards the view,
outside, of a disused marketplace,
overlooked memorial plaque,
closed shops, timetables, graveyard,

and at the street's far end,
beyond disused factory structures,
its brick canyon screeching
with seagulls: a post-industrial sky.
Cars briefly trouble the flyover.
Brown tourist signage points
to 'Brontë country' and 'Wuthering Heights'.

Miles Away

As the bus never came,
after lunch beneath the water tower,
we're out walking on the Downs,
making long, rectangular diversions around
a dozen Sunday football games
to take a path I've not taken before,
along the Gorge's rim, beside Sea Walls.

Only, despite the ready evidence,
our lazy talk in breeze-burnt air,
each urgent footfall's sound –
it's as if I'm not all there,
distracted by cross-hatched branches
against blurred skies, sheer drops
into perspectives of a different terrain:
inland chalk deposits, sheep tracks, scrub,
a view of hills bisected by the London train.

So much for moving on or growing away.
Somehow I'm always partly on the stairs,
from where you'll see gardens and garages
gathering to the cement works' cloud.

And yes, here I am, reversing
into another Cold War: campaigns
of silence, hissed regrets
and disputes over borders
that won't come right.
Whatever I missed before
flashes like torches through these trees –
which would soon, had we known it,
succumb to infestation, Dutch Elm disease.

I'm looking out for god knows what –
starting pistol, seeds being sown –
when all this happened many years ago.

Coming back, or coming round,
there's something being said,
a piece of family news or weather patterns'
unfathomable changes like incremental doubts.
I've got some catching up to do.
Or were you pointing something out?
That player back from the touchline, say,
who's off the ball but charges up the pitch
to rejoin the game, regain his ground.

Changing the Geography

Songlines map vast tracts down under
but your tracks through town are just
the paths of habit. Walking to work,
these are the faces you ignore every day,
more or less a little late.

You're not hauling yourself along
the thread of some dreamtime story,
only, crossing this square's clean slate,
you were almost thrown off course
by the geography's changes this week.

Was this the tree where you took shelter,
not so much from unexpected weather
as from people you might have known?
You were backed up against its trunk
and she was, simply, in your arms.

You keep closely to the other path
but this story's traces stick:
late-night bar, taxi rank, statue,
the fake ritzy ballroom of that hotel.
A whole new set of landmarks insist
you're moving through an unfamiliar city.

How far have you strayed? Are you lost?
You might be. Perhaps. And glad of it.
Not completely off the map
but finding it's been re-drawn,
trusting a new guide, seeing it all
laid out in different light.

Performance Art in Private Gardens

Twenty years on from very nearly reaching out
of a musty festival sleeping bag
and knowing how you might have felt,
having more than smart words between us,
we finally embrace like old friends.

Under trees, the gaze of connoisseurs,
your second husband laments the sorrows
of a distant nation. You nurse your child and mine
look simply defeated. There is nothing needs be said
about vicissitudes of fate, divergent paths
or other convenient fictions. The selves
we could have been don't even ghost
the chestnut shadows squaring off
these private gardens.

Somehow we have steered out into the world,
losing touch – and will again – amongst
uncertain geographies: streets, estrangements,
postings, airports. What would have been
and gone by now, it's hard to say.
Arboreal penumbras overlap the space
he's made. And just for a moment it's clear.
We're playing with ideas, we are.

The Chopin Question

Why, for example, should it come
as any surprise to find
that, having watched *The Pianist*,
the Warsaw Ghetto decimations,
there is a jar of *Smak* beetroot
on my kitchen shelf,
or that in a shop's stuffed racks
a Polish masthead sits flush
with Italian, German, French?

Was this any reason to reach up
to the lid of the piano and pick
the first sheet music to come to hand?
Then flinch, as if it had been charged,
like that boy in O-level physics
who kept his hand too long
on the Van de Graaff generator?

There's nothing of fate about it.
In whose interest would it be
that I chanced on Chopin's *Preludes*?
How could that make life better or worse?

Egdon Road

Some nights, quite late, the lighted corner shop
sells chocolate bars, toilet rolls and milk.

The long lane stretches to a café-bar or flats,
depending on which way you look down it.

Drivers on a crash course lunge at junctions;
houses back away between the streetlamps.

A lone bat barrel-rolls along front gardens,
a pipistrelle, perhaps, that tracks you home.

The Three-Day Melt

After waiting the week
for a damaged gutter's steady drip,
it starts to beat an old tattoo.
And we are amongst the few,
digging out our neighbourly slush,
metal offered to the melting ridge,
and thinking ourselves heroic.

Glossed by sun-tormented snow,
the street achieves a sheen,
like a hotel foyer magazine,
before it hardens, greys,
maculate as newsprint.
Here are the furrows we made,
footfalls disappearing.

Already we are forgetting
the claustrophobic days,
beating around the bush
to clear negotiable ways
back to the ordinary rush.

Out of suspension now,
the accelerating hours
push on; clouds clear;
and we can no longer mark time –
grateful, at least, for not
having to watch every step.

So Close

Way off track among brick-paved streets
of a post-recession housing estate –
his short cut proving nothing of the sort –
we check our relative positions
like reconnaissance pilots homing in
on hypothetical targets.

So much for senses of direction.
By still-unfinished apartment blocks,
billboards obstruct the view with offers
of how we might expect to live:
an abundance of appliances,
were we equipped to use them.
And I am at a loss in front
of regeneration zones,
a lack of discernible routes between
trompe l'oeil plasma video screens.

You, love, are heading back elsewhere.
Commuters gather to a swarm
at the station's barriered entrances.
Is this how far we've come –
milling, distanced, but in the same crowd?
Here's the phone again. It's you.
Turn round. You'll see.
I'm only these few feet away.

Found in the River

Sometimes, approaching light
occurs beyond terraces, cranes,
the silvery distance
of the dredged-at sea.
Ducks bob and weave,
and the rest rots down
to pub talk, postcodes,
pads of matted weed.

From Rochester to Rotherhithe,
the river's urban bucolic:
intrusion, expulsion of tides
between warehouse developments,
bearded wooden piles,
it brings in, drags out
infertile salmon, stinging brine.

That man had just about enough.
Bewhiskered, posed at the tiller,
he takes the reach, his wife
and children arranged
for the photo on deck.
The boat he'd bought at Herne Bay;
London he'd read of in Dickens,
its backdrop's derricked outline.

Between these capital silhouettes,
I can just imagine
hawkers stalling outside his shop
or Veneerings peeled off
to chat at social functions.
He's sailed straight into a novel,
a saturated city.

Look back from a ferry nosing west
and it fits: the ill-judged passions,
fraternal rivalry, gist
of great-grandfather's plot.
Distracted by business,
by making ends meet,
he stands here taking stock
while Gaffer Hexham
punts out from the shore,
reaches down, collecting bodies,
and then pushes onwards, searching for more.

The Breakage Suite

Whenever you came home, there
was always something to mend
or tinker with: washing machine,
coal boiler, unheralded mod cons.
Rewired, retuned, a radio
cut in on your modest *ta-da*.
Nothing went back to the shop.
Spare parts that would come in handy
one day cluttered chests of drawers.

Somewhere around this time
there would have been rumours
of strikes, a change of government.
You visited the Ideal Home,
brought back the textured sofa
we sat on through the power cuts.

*

It was only just beginning.
The soft taps momentarily halt
and my daughter calls me in
to diagnose frozen windows
on her laptop's screen.
A glitch, a virus, I've no idea.
Warranties expired the other week.
Together we wait on an error report.

*

It's the closest I've come
to turning back: Euston Station
through the window of a cab.
As if fifty minutes up the line
there'd be spark plugs in the sink
and your exasperation.

There's nothing I could do.
What kind of fix were you in?
The glass and steel remain
inscrutable as circuit board.

Under skies that thin to brightness
by this concrete plaza's to-and-froing,
I might have been speaking
of watch repairs. Only now,
as time changes gear,
I have other things to mind,
another elsewhere into which we're going.

Fenlanders

Perfectly flat source
of glass-half-empty wisdom
(*You never gain without you lose*),
these drains and fenland ooze;
unbroken horizontals
bred smallholders quick
to silence, feuds.
Cousins, not on speaking terms,
learnt allegiances, who was who,
precise degrees of indifference to use
in the family's every orbit.

A lack of generosity in nature, then,
accounting for a hardness of heart?
Well, yes, there was that – breeding fruit
and veg from plots that felt the brunt
of poor winters, North Sea winds,
relentless, giddying skies.
No wonder they took the dim view,
were adamant they knew what they knew,
distrust of water, close observation
of changes, levels and rules,
the fragile treachery of things,
a closed world better off for keeping closed.

From here, though, also, eccentricities of will:
great-grandfather who made do
and the most out of left-overs,
sticks, old hat. Always on the loose,
ditch-strider, habitual trespasser,
or, back home, his having to explain,
if anyone should ask, why the swan
he'd killed was better called a goose.
Such stamina for living on the hoof:
as if each morning, bent-double and running,
he was tempting snipers to shoot him down,
 which on such open ground they could have easily done.

Ellerker Gardens

Learning to count to six, out of habit,
as, standing in Ellerker Gardens,
you'd watch, each night, the fire curtain
draw across the roofs of London;
you were listening for a silence in that storm,
the absence of an unexploded bomb.

Could you be so absorbed you'd not recall
an insect bite, a broken date,
the instinct for survival which ensured
you kept well clear of the house
until your father had been and gone?
Just heroism of the ordinary sort

among lattices of blown-out beams
would see you safe, in some way at least,
as you searched through the blackout and blast
for whatever fate was lying, waiting,
cradled in the sixth silence.

The Stone Platoon

How else to look at this fountain
with adjacent memorial statues?
Drizzle's left droplets finding paths
through embossed verdigris,
such-and-such a name who fell.
I'm not close enough to make
more of others' particular loss
in whichever battle or campaign.
The stone platoon endures
inclement weather,
bayonets fixed at thickening air.

Remembrance Sunday every year,
we'd stand by our indifference,
dragooned Boy Scouts in the breeze
which furled around a cenotaph,
putting up with it, out of respect –
although, eventually, out of respect,
we'd surrender to goose bumps,
laughter and knocked knees.

Here, then, historians gather,
deciphering epitaphs
for losses on some foreign field.
What could it be to them
who died, who came home,
in any event, who won?
Their silence affects some care.
Under sun-split skies,
they line up for a photograph
with those who, *in memoriam* there,
did the best they could have done.

The Air Display

Jetstream mirage and the taste of kerosene
is how it might start across the field,
or a Hawker Hunter hanging on a stall turn,
its chevron tailfin roundel against clouds.
Armed with bulbous candyfloss,
we're walking between disputes,
provenance issues, these tanks
too often repaired, no longer 'authentic'.
Redundant fighters' afterburners sear
the early afternoon like rough nostalgia,
aerobatics over middle England.

And still it is easier to find a name
for Venom, Tempest, Fury
or how we might be expected to feel
about splintered tree-lines,
sand-bursts across that combat zone,
than for patterns of thought
in these actually occurring vapour trails
which backdrop one last fly-past:
impervious Spitfire, engine growling,
over woods and out of the sun.

Wearing Thin

Going home, with decisions unmade
and threats of further paperwork,
you're jostling for position
at a crossing point, taking
the lights' delay as reluctance,
the pavement for a starting grid.
As if a whole town could do its best
to hold you back.
Or that stained-glass triptych
of a church's nominal saints
had been set there to laud it
over epidemic rumours,
determined indignation.

Out in the river, a cormorant's neck
snags the current. What might be
flickers across lifestyle smiles
on emphatic development hoardings.
A bank declares its lending rate,
intent on your interest,
or diverts you to
career-changing posters,
temp agency chances.

As red turns to green,
you've almost reached the other side
before you're pulled up short
by a misread fashion headline:
You Are What You Were.

Disrupted Sleep

Out of a dream of a day by an ornamental lake
where, amongst rhododendra, my father
appears to be offering advice, or his hand
on my elbow at least, I'm fiercely awake,
insomniac between sweat-drenched sheets
and a three a.m. silence that gives way
to cross-city sirens and, closer,
dallying homecomers' chat in the street.

Your absence makes me fonder.
Half-mad with deferred regrets,
as if here in your unindented pillow
were everything we might have been
or what little you've left behind,
the next hour labours like a week.

Back on the Shelf

Almost on the brink of a gorge
you might be surprised
by a pair of shoes on the shelf
of a closing secondhand shop.
Winter dusk undoes the sky's
complexities: in this light
all cars are turning grey
or home. The straps glint,
sequinned, as they did
in the foyer of the Hotel Illyria.
Among the bay's tipped rocks
the plumes of smoke from barbecues
are like a taxi's departure.
Someone else will wear your shoes.

Observation Carriage

Amongst tall blank walls
        of the uncompleted shopping centre,
birds lunge and weave and dive
        like poor wee scraps
of conversation. The train
        leaves Lille, half-empty or half-full,
despite its good connections.
        What was that?
You've no more strength for rows
        of shingled terraces
than for marginal prospects,
        ticketing options, the shape
your life's assuming,
        as fixed as the contours
        of this old blue hat?

Deep in trees that flank
        another model village,
a ruined hunting lodge
        or, perhaps, a hide –
you'd do better
        not to take it so hard
that somewhere up ahead
        there'll be a bus held up
at an untimely level crossing.
In spring, elsewhere, you were occupied.
Or at least no longer avoiding
        late-for-school children's faces
        breathing steam on glass.

Playing Piano for the Folks

Somehow notes came, and some relief,
in that Sunday afternoon parlour
just below the Mason-Dixon Line,
Chopin simplified, for their ears only,
under a stuttering ceiling fan.

Barely able to reach the grand piano's
smooth-worn pedals, you skipped
beats, skewed chords, fluffed
plangent minors, and would
blame, had you thought of it,
air-pressure or too-prompt applause.

She, though, sweltered
in the heat elsewhere,
tangential to another life,
moving along these swampy margins:
girl on a swing with view of ferns
and closing, thickening skies.

In a moment, there she was,
running towards the house,
percussive hail on the porch roof,
the tree-branch cracking,
lightning irreversibly struck.

Catching the Drift

Mist-wreathed skiff masts lie at odds.
'The well-to-do,' you say,
and nod towards a terraced foreshore.
Collared by its spectral bridge, the bay's incursion
narrows to a creek, these tongues of sand.
You hand out cigarettes.
The boats kick and slap at the pier end.
What deed, what possession
stakes claims for those
who weekend at the sea's edge?

Only here, on this shack's uneven planks,
the morning's steeped in diesel fumes,
and flies, perplexed by angling lures,
like grounds for battlers' complaints,
seethe on fish-heads lopped for bait.
That's not your way. We push off,
grab oars, strike, and catch the drift
as it squirls through fallen branches,
knots of weed, the sure-footed bridge
and its concrete stanchions,
then thickens to an estuary.

If the jetstreams
unfurling north and east
register as promises, promises
made at one time to yourself,
there's not a sign you feel betrayed,
here beyond the holiday homes,
at the start, the very start of open water.

Almost There

Beyond the canalised river's curving banks,
the old town teeters on a rocky brink,
or so it seems from where we're standing
only these few minutes after stepping down
an avenue gloomy with plane trees.
Houses front up to the street
and everyone we pass is studiously indifferent.

It's August and the castle, we assume,
is thick with precipitate tourists. A girl
strains hard at a cigarette and hands
around a can of beer. The river
stays determinedly grey, no matter
how we look at it. Up ahead,
there's a pink-sprayed underpass.

This might be how we re-enter Europe,
back, at last, with pizzerias, the trams
and subjunctive clauses. A not
wholly unexpected arrangement
of pensioners with dogs and teenagers
deployed along the banks
of an Austro-Hungarian waterway.

Relieved at this closeness to home,
small, familiar indications,
a temperate change in the weather,
we almost fail to grasp
the graffiti's fresh insistence –
'Freedom and unity now!' –
or the distance still to travel.

Allotment Poem

In the interests of making amends,
I'll trudge this hill with rough implements
and dig into the earth. Spring creaks
its grey-greenery, stumped cabbage stalks,
and horizons loosen into a smile
which almost hurts from its precision.

Now connections ache so much
amongst the groundsel patches.
Lines beg to differ. How else
to regard these rhubarb tips sprouting
from compost? Or the spindrift-may
that crests upsweeping breeze?

Still such care to be taken (to find
and not expect). I'm staring at my shoes,
while over and above this valley's
unambitious public transport routes
hen harriers jockey on the thermals.
Poets, their words, ghost cemetery yews,
and mushrooms slip in between my feet.

Long-term Forecast

On the day of the street party,
a cold front's edges came no closer,
draped their threat across the gorge,
suggestive backdrop to the wrong scene.
It seemed as if I'd understood
our economic fix –
although when trying to explain
I could only clutch at
fiscal questions, distant wars,
situations out of my hands.

On the corner bar's terrace,
there's football disappointments
to discuss, an afternoon's loss,
and some pretty girl (or plain)
amongst pained, shuffling joggers,
anxiety – or other mood –
hidden by her shades.

Yes, the day the bunting flew,
cloud strata stalled,
I was half-convinced.
Gloss paint, sawdust smell,
domestic renovations –
things weren't so bad
on hold as neighbours strolled
through intermittent sunlight.

On the corner bar's terrace,
the conversation's turned
to passport legislation,
their 'coming over here',
and respect for the chancers
whose state we're in.

Newspaper sheets ruck up
against a wall: 'scandal', 'power'
and photos of our latest duchess
scuffle into commentary.
Across the street,
the auctioneer's hammer
snaps down on every 'Going, going, gone'.
The cold front's stand-off lasts another hour.

The Centre, Friday

This is not a place to be in at a loss:
you need wits and cash about you.
And I am a different person on these streets,
adjusting pace and expression to how
it might be possible not to stand at odds.
Common ground amongst predictable gridlock
is reduced to a concrete plaza with fountains,
Bible bashers, benches, rubbish bins:
whatever each complains of when we'll be home.

There's a long way to go before that.
The waterfront bellows with stag parties;
tourists affront lovers sequestered at wharf's edge.
Negotiating the overspill from franchised bars,
there seems to be some hope for separate peace.
At the outset of Friday night, the cordon's drawn up:
helicopter flashlights splash along the harbour.

It's not the whole story. On the corner
by the swing bridge's worn-through asphalt tiles,
the leaf-clogged puddles on harbourside cobbles,
you were almost in danger of kicking away
a used condom's rubbery squiggle:
sign at least that, in this intoxicating air,
someone was tempted to believe
love was somewhere near.

Portishead

All through her second wedding, your sister carried white lilies.
She chose Psalm 23 and we duly mumbled
'The Lord is my shepherd, I shall not want',
thinking this is more like a funeral
and trying not to giggle at the serious bits.
You dug me in the ribs and said,
with more feeling than you meant,
that this is what passes for life in Portishead.

Outside – we nipped out for a fag during 'Abide With Me',
tip-toeing past weeping aunts and teenage sons
in suits they'd bought for work experience
(a row of bulging parcels waiting for collection) –
outside you breathed again and then you said
how glad you were you'd escaped
what passes for life in Portishead.

And when you kissed me in the graveyard
with its blots of dead confetti like giant flakes of dandruff,
I was thinking: Yes, thank God, thank God,
if it hadn't been for this town's deep chill,
its icy politeness and evening classes,
its Sunday lunch drinks and over-cooked roasts,
the dismal rain on the Lake Grounds of a Saturday night,
if it hadn't been for the gossip which spread
like a bushfire when you dyed your hair red
and started hanging out with unsuitable types
who played in punk bands like Chaos UK
or limped along the high street on farting Lambrettas –
if it hadn't been for this town's desire
to disapprove of all it didn't understand,

you'd never have run for Cornwall and the sea,
you'd never have run for a place of your own
and you'd never have run into me.
In the doorway of the church, I almost smiled and I almost said:
there are so many reasons I'm grateful
for what passes for life in Portishead.

Two Rivers Press has been publishing in and about Reading since 1994. Founded by the artist Peter Hay (1951–2003), the press continues to delight readers, local and further afield, with its varied list of individually designed, thought-provoking books.